TEN
COMMANDMENTS
FOR
BEGINNERS

BY
DAVID W. NEW
ATTORNEY AT LAW

A POCKET PUBLICATION®
BETHESDA, MARYLAND

The Ten Commandments For Beginners
Copyright © 2004 David W. New
ISBN 0-9721333-4-8

David W. New is proud to present this publication,
The Ten Commandments For Beginners in celebration
of the 350th anniversary of the arrival of the first
community of Jews to settle in North America--------
(1654 - 2004).

Published by:
A Pocket Publication/David W. New.

Printed in the United States of America.

This publication is dedicated to
Pastor Robert L. Schenck
of FaithandAction.org

For his work for the
Ten Commandments.

"My people are destroyed for lack of knowledge.
Because you have rejected knowledge,
I also will reject you from being priest for Me;
Because you have forgotten the law of your God,
I also will forget your children."

Hosea 4:6

ABOUT THE AUTHOR:

David W. New is an attorney in the Washington, D.C. area. He received his JD degree from the Georgetown University Law Center in 1989. In 1978, David received a B.S. degree in Accounting and a B.A. degree in Economics from Humboldt State University in Arcata, CA. David has pursued post-graduate studies at the Air Force Institute of Technology at Wright-Patterson AFB in Ohio. David studied Biblical Hebrew and NT Greek at Harvard University. In January 2003, David received an honorary Doctor of Divinity degree from the Methodist Episcopal Church USA.

If you would like more copies of this booklet: *The Ten Commandments For Beginners* visit: www.mytencommandments.us

OTHER PUBLICATIONS BY DAVID W. NEW:
The New Testament For Beginners
The Constitution For Beginners
The First Amendment And The Bill Of Rights For Beginners
Religious Freedom In America For Beginners

STUDENTS, WOULD YOU LIKE TO WEAR A TEN COMMANDMENTS T SHIRT TO SCHOOL?
Contact Evelyn Bradley at HelpSaveAmerica.com, P.O. Box 59147, Norwalk, CA 90650 or by phone at 562-863-7783 or at PetitionGodBless@aol.com

" . . . looking for the blessed hope and glorious appearing of our great God and Savior Jesus Christ."

Titus 2:13

TABLE OF CONTENTS

THE TEN COMMANDMENTS FOR BEGINNERS

What would the world be like if everyone honored the Ten Commandments? Suppose people suddenly began to follow the Ten Commandments, how would that affect your life? Would it matter if they only made a good faith effort to keep the Commandments? Absolutely Yes! If we took the Ten Commandments as seriously as we take making money, the quality of life on this planet would improve for everyone. Even if we only made a good faith effort to keep the Ten Commandments, our world would experience the greatest rebirth since the Creation. We could even taste a piece of heaven itself. This is what God's moral law can do for us. God has said that His Word never returns to Him void. If America returned to God's moral law, this nation would enjoy the greatest spiritual and material prosperity the world has ever seen. Obviously, there are powerful groups like the ACLU who would not like to see this happen. But it could happen. It is doubtful that the nations of the world will ever be interested in the Ten Commandments, but thankfully millions of Americans are. Many of us believe that the blessings America has received will continue only if we honor God's moral law. God has promised a rich reward to any nation that honors His laws. "Righteousness exalts a nation. But sin is a reproach to any people" Solomon said. Prov. 14:34. If *"We The People"* return to the moral and spiritual foundations of our Constitution, then it is certain that God will exalt America before the nations of the world. In addition, there is a rich reward for anyone who honors His laws as well. If you and I were the only people on earth interested in the Ten Commandments, God would bless us just the same. Our lives would prosper. Our minds and bodies would be blessed. We would become the kind of people God wants us to be. There is a story in the Gospels about a woman who had a horrible disease in her body. One day she reached out and touched the fringes of Jesus' clothes. These fringes which Jesus wore were very special. They were a symbol of God's commandments which include the Ten Commandments. Jewish men were commanded by God to wear fringes with their clothes. See Num. 15:37-41. When she reached out and touched the fringes, the symbol of God's commandments, she instantly was healed in her body. Dear reader, if you reach out and touch the fringes of His garments, your life will be blessed as well. This is God's promise to you. Note 1.

The purpose of this booklet is to provide the reader with a quick and easy way to understand the Ten Commandments. I assume the reader knows little or nothing about these precious jewels. However, if you can read at a junior high reading level, you can easily understand the lessons in this booklet. The grammar is basic. New and unusual words are defined. This booklet was written primarily for young people, but older readers can enjoy these lessons as well. There are five lessons in this booklet. The first lesson provides the reader with the Jewish view of the Ten Commandments. The second lesson explains the meaning of each of the Ten Commandments. In this lesson we will answer the question: "What Have the Ten Commandments Done for Me?" Here we learn the countless ways we have benefitted from the Ten Commandments. The second lesson is the most important lesson in this booklet. In the third lesson, we will learn about the great contributions the Ten Commandments have made to American law. For example, consider the words *Equal Justice Under Law* which appear on the outside of the U.S. Supreme Court building. Most Americans are unaware that the concept of *Equal Justice Under Law* is a religious concept. It did not originate from secularism. The Ten Commandments taught us that everyone is equal under the law. The fourth lesson will answer this question: Should Religious Values Influence the U.S. Constitution? Finally, we will consider the issue of the display of the Ten Commandments on public property and Judge Roy Moore. I am confident that the reader will have a much better understanding of the Ten Commandments after reading this booklet. Let us begin.

The Jewish Surprise!

The Jewish view of the Ten Commandments is different from what most people might expect. Rabbinic Judaism teaches that only the Jews must keep the Ten Commandments. Rabbinic Judaism refers to the teachings of the rabbis which began at the time of Jesus and continues to the present day. They believe that God commanded only the Jewish people to keep the Ten Commandments. Rabbinic Judaism teaches that the Gentiles should obey the "Noahide Laws," which are similar to the Ten Commandments. See Gen. 9:1-6. Jewish tradition says that these laws have been binding on all humanity from the days of Adam. In the Jewish tradition, the Noahide Laws consist of seven laws of God which apply to all humankind. They are as follows:

1) Do not worship idols, 2) Do not blaspheme the name of God, 3) Establish courts of justice, 4) Do not kill, 5) Do not commit adultery, 6) Do not rob and 7) Do not eat flesh that has been cut from a living animal. Note 2.

However, there is another view. Not all Jews believe the Ten Commandments apply only to the Jewish people. Many believe the Ten Commandments are a universal moral code that apply to everyone. They believe this because of where God gave the Ten Commandments. The Ten Commandments were given to Moses the Lawgiver in the desert of Mount Sinai. In Bible times, the desert was considered to be a "no man's land." Many Jews believe that the reason God gave the Ten Commandments to Moses in the desert was to teach us that His moral laws apply to everyone. By giving the Ten Commandments in "no man's land" and not in Israel, God is saying that His moral laws are not limited to the Jewish people. I agree with this view. There can be no question that the Ten Commandments are special. The Bible says that God personally wrote these commandments with His own finger. Note 3.

What Have the Ten Commandments Done for Me?

The Ten Commandments are listed in the Book of Exodus 20: 2-17 and in Deuteronomy 5: 6-21. We will limit our study to the list found in the Book of Exodus. By tradition the Ten Commandments are divided into two groups of five. The first five commandments concern our duties to God and our parents. The second five commandments concern our duties to society in general. Some people wonder why our duties to our parents are listed with our duty to God. There is a good reason for this. Our parents teach us about God. Our father teaches us about God's justice and power. Our mother teaches us about God's love and tenderness. Both attributes of God are essential. Additionally, our parents teach us how to live in society. They teach us what is good and bad behavior. Thus, the Fifth Commandment, to honor your father and your mother is a pivotal commandment. Our parents are our bridge to God and to society in general. The key to a strong nation is the family. A nation which honors the institution of the family in its laws will need fewer prisons.

My God: The First Commandment

"I am the Lord your God, who brought you out of the land of Egypt, out of the house of bondage. You shall have no other gods before Me."   Ex. 20:2-3

The First Commandment is the most important commandment. We will study it in two parts.

Part 1

"I am the Lord your God . . ."
                                        Ex. 20:2

The moral authority for the Ten Commandments is God. The key words are: "I am the Lord your God . . ." There is no higher authority in the Universe than God. Absolutely none. Consequently, His law supercedes all human law. For example, if the government passed a law which said murder is ok. This law is immoral and must not be obeyed. God's law says, "You shall not murder." God's law must be obeyed because it supercedes human law. On the Day of Judgment, if you plead "innocent" to the charge of murder because the government said it was ok, God will not accept your plea. His law comes first and we must obey it.

By far, the most important words in the Ten Commandments are: "Lord" and "God." These two words teach us about God's character and His divine attributes. It is very important to know who God is. Unless we know who God is, we cannot know who we are. We can only understand our place in the Universe if we know God. In other words, God helps us to "make sense" out of the world. The word "Lord" is the most important word in the Bible. The word Lord comes from four letters in the Hebrew alphabet YHWH. These four letters are known as the Tetragrammaton. Tetra is from the Greek meaning "four" and gramma means "letters," or four letters. The tetragrammaton has been interpreted in the Bible as "I AM WHO I AM" or "I WILL BE WHAT I WILL BE." See Ex. 3:14. This word teaches us that the Lord is One. There is only One Lord. There aren't two lords, three lords, or many lords. There is only One Lord. The belief that the Lord is One or that God is One is known as monotheism. Mono means "one" and theos means "god." Monotheism teaches that there is only One God. On a list of the top five ideas upon which Western Civilization is built upon, monotheism tops the list! No concept is more important to Western thinking than monotheism. Our concept of *Equal Justice Under Law* for example came from monotheism. The next most important word in the Bible is "God" which is from the Hebrew word "Elohim." This is the word used in Genesis 1:1, "In the beginning God created the heavens and the earth." Elohim refers to God as the Creator. There is only One Lord who is also God the Creator of the Universe. The Lord is God. The Lord is One. *Thus, the moral foundation of the Ten Commandments is monotheism.* Note 4.

How the Ten Commandments
Led to the Rise of Modern Science

Why is it so important to think of God as One? Why is the Ten Commandments' teaching of monotheism so important? There are many reasons. For now let's consider just one area, modern science. Modern science would not be possible but for the influence of the Ten Commandments. To understand why this is true, let's shift gears for a moment and pretend we are going back in time to thousands of years ago, to a time when polytheism dominated the world. The word poly means "many" and theos means "god." In the ancient world, the people believed in many gods. They were polytheist. The gods were everywhere. Every time you moved from one kingdom to another you came to a new god. If you moved from one part of a city to another part, you came to a new god. Additionally, some of these gods were "in" every thing as well. A tree had a god. A rock had a god. A river had a god. Indeed, the river was a god. The tree was a god and so was the rock. In effect, nature was god. This view of god is called pantheism. Pan means "all" and theos means "god." God is IN every thing or god is in nature. Consequently, people in the ancient world worshiped birds, goats, cats, snakes and bugs, etc. This was the world before the rise of monotheism and the Ten Commandments. Even today, polytheism continues in India and in many other places. Many New Age religions in the United States are nothing more than ancient pantheism repackaged. Now ask yourself this question, what effect did these ideas about god have on science? A LOT. The main obstacle to science in the ancient world was false religion. False religion got in the way of science and scientific study. Consider one example. In many high school biology classes, the time will come when the students will be asked to dissect a frog. Frogs are dissected to learn about anatomy and other things. In the ancient world this would not have been possible. The theologians of the day would have considered the dissection of a frog to be blasphemy because the frog is a god, and gods don't like to be dissected. It hurts! Now multiply this one example a million times a million. There were an unlimited number of ways that the religious thinking of the people held science back. When you read the great thinkers of the ancient world, it is clear that what was holding them back was their false religion! The way they thought about the gods got in the way of sound logical thinking.

Now let's introduce a new way of thinking called monotheism. This new thinking was introduced by Moses the Lawgiver. He made a new revolutionary statement which changed the world forever. He said: "In the beginning God created the heavens and the earth." Gen. 1:1. When these words were written 3,500 years ago, they were radical. For here Moses was saying that God was *separate* from the

Creation. God existed before the Creation and God was separate from the Creation. Before the physical Creation existed there was only God. This concept had a profound impact on science. Since God and the Creation were separate then by definition this means that nature was not god. Bugs, goats, trees and rivers are not gods because God preceded their existence. As soon as we learned that God was separated from the Creation, true scientific study became possible. By separating God from the Creation, you separate the theologian from the scientist. In effect, monotheism frees the scientist. Consequently, you can dissect all the frogs you want to for your scientific study as long as you are nice about it! lol. The scientific study of nature was not possible until nature was no longer worshiped as a god. Our solar system could not be understood until monotheism dethroned the planets as gods. Monotheism is the reason modern science excelled in the West. Modern science advanced in the Western world because our culture accepted the concept of monotheism as taught by Moses.

Admittedly, even in the West, science had a difficult time. Copernicus and Galileo are just two examples. But the rise of modern science in the West was inevitable with the adoption of monotheism. Genesis 1:1 is the most profound scientific statement ever made in history. These words made modern science possible.

"What Have the Ten Commandments Done for Me?" You have already benefitted from the Ten Commandments a million times over and you don't even know it. If you do not believe that rocks, squirrels and birds are gods, you owe it to the influence of the Ten Commandments! Essentially, the Ten Commandments allow us to think *logically, clearly and scientifically.* It is a bit ironic that there are some scientists who deny the existence of the One God and yet they think like a monotheist--and they don't even know they are doing it.

Part 2

"You shall have no other gods before Me."
Ex. 20:3

The English translation of this verse is a bit confusing. It appears to teach that "other gods" are real. This of course is not true. There is only One God and none other exist. All the gods that people think exist are imaginary. A better translation of this verse is "You shall not recognize the gods of others before My presence." This is much closer to the intent of the commandment. We live before God's all seeing Eye all the time. Therefore, our behavior should reflect this understanding. This means that idols and false gods should not be in our homes or in our thoughts. We must not follow the ways of the world and think that nature is god or that animals are gods. There is One God and none other. This commandment not only applies to idols which we can see and touch but it can apply to anything that we put ahead of God as well. If there is anything that is more important to us than God, we have in effect made a "god" out of it. This can be a house, a car, money or even a loved one. Nothing must take the place of God in our hearts. God must be first in our life. If we put God first then everything else in our life will fall neatly into place. Jesus said, "But seek first the kingdom of God and His righteousness, and all these things (food, clothing, shelter etc.) shall be added to you." Matt. 6:33. One of the biggest mistakes people make in life is not getting their priorities straight. What have the Ten Commandments done for me? They taught me that God should come first in my life.

My God: The Second Commandment

"You shall not make for yourself a carved image–any likeness of anything that is in heaven above, or that is in the earth beneath, or that is in the water under the earth . . ."
                                                        Ex. 20:4-6

In the ancient world, people would take a piece of wood and make an idol out of it. They would put it some place special and worship it. In some cases, they would even offer human sacrifices to it. They were in bondage to superstition and ignorance. When the Second Commandment was written, this was how primitive societies behaved. Thankfully, our society has progressed beyond superstition and ignorance. The influence of the Ten Commandments on our modern culture is unmistakable. People no longer bow down to wooden idols because of this commandment. It is amazing how much people fail to understand how important the Ten Commandments are. What have the Ten Commandments done for me? They gave me a society in which people are not in bondage to superstition and backward ideas.

My God: The Third Commandment

"You shall not take the name of the Lord your God in vain, for the Lord will not hold him guiltless who takes His name in vain."
Ex. 20:7

If you want to show respect for God, show respect for His Name. When the Bible was written, names had a far greater importance than they do now. Today, we name our children after a relative or just because we like the sound of a particular name, but when the Bible was written, the giving of a name was very serious business. It was believed that a person's name represented the character or personality of that individual. So a person's name was very important. Interestingly, even in today's popular culture certain names have a symbolic meaning just like they did in Bible times. For example, the name "George Washington" stands for liberty and freedom while the name "Adolf Hitler" stands for evil and death. Additionally, people received a new name when they experienced some great event in their life. This happened to Jacob in Genesis Chapter 32. Here Jacob had a life changing experience with the "Angel of the Lord." He received a new name because of it. Jacob's new name was "Israel" or "the prince that prevails with God." Most likely Jacob met with Jesus Christ who appeared to him as the "Angel of the Lord."

If human names are important, then God's Name YHWH is infinitely more important. Indeed, God's Name is more important than the Creation itself. For God's personal name, YHWH, preceded the Creation of the Universe. YHWH or as it is sometimes called "Jehovah" means "I AM THAT I AM." It means that God is eternal, omniscient and omnipotent. God is eternal because He is not limited by time. He has no past, present or future. God is omniscient because He is all knowing. God has perfect knowledge of everything. God is omnipotent because He is all powerful. There is no higher power in the Universe than God.

What does it mean to take God's Name in vain? It means to use God's Name lightly or casually. This includes blasphemy but it can mean a lot more than that. It means being disrespectful to God through His name. Having respect for God is important. People who do not respect God do not respect themselves or other people. What have the Ten Commandments done for me? They taught me that by having respect for God's Name, I will have respect for myself and for other people.

My Creator: The Fourth Commandment

"Remember the Sabbath day, to keep it holy." Ex. 20:8

The Book of Genesis Chapter 2 says that after God finished creating the heavens and the earth, He rested on the seventh day and blessed it. Thus, the Sabbath was a day to acknowledge God as the Creator. Gentiles name their days of the week after pagan gods. The words Monday, Wednesday, Thursday, etc. all came from pagan gods. Jews do not do this. The Jews follow the Bible. They number their days of the week. They number them relative to the Sabbath Day. Thus, the first day, the second day, the third day, etc. are numbered relative to the seventh day, the Sabbath Day just like the Bible. The Jews want to live each day of the week with the Sabbath always in view in order to honor God as the Creator. In addition, there is another reason to keep the Sabbath. The Bible says God rested on the seventh day. When we honor the Sabbath Day, we are resting from our labor like God. Thus, we affirm that we are not slaves to our work. This rest also provides us an opportunity to think about God and to meditate on Him. The Sabbath reminds us that there is more to life than work. What have the Ten Commandments done for me? They gave me a day of rest to honor God as the Creator and to rest like Him.

At one time, Sabbath laws were very popular in the United States. If one member of the U.S.

Supreme Court is correct, 49 of the 50 states had a law originating from the Fourth Commandment. Note 5. Thomas Jefferson, who authored the phrase "separation of church and state" was very interested in the Sabbath as well. When he was a member of the Virginia legislature, he personally wrote a Sabbath law. It was called *"A Bill for Punishing Disturbers of Religious Worship and Sabbath Breakers."* This law required the citizens of Virginia not to work on the Sabbath Day. If they did, they could be fined. Jefferson did not succeed in getting his Sabbath law passed, but many years later a friend of his did. His name was James Madison, the "Father of the Constitution." When Madison was a member of the Virginia legislature, he got Jefferson's Sabbath law passed for him. This occurred on November 27, 1786. Interestingly, six months after Madison got the Sabbath law passed, he was in Philadelphia attending the constitutional convention. Madison had a leading role in writing the Constitution of the United States. Apparently, neither Jefferson nor Madison felt that Sabbath laws violated the separation of church and state. They did not believe it was wrong for the government to acknowledge God. Note 6. Of course, the Sabbath that Jefferson and Madison wrote about was kept on Sunday. Since New Testament times, Christians have kept the first day of the week. See Acts 20:7. Christians worship on the first day of the week because they believe Jesus Christ rose from the dead on this day. The first day of the week is a celebration of God as the Creator as well. However, in this instance the creation celebrated is a spiritual creation. The spiritual creation is the New Birth which every Christian receives in Jesus Christ. See 2 Cor. 5:17. Christians also believe the first day is a day of rest as well. Here however the rest is in the person of Jesus Christ. See Matt. 11:28-30.

My Family: The Fifth Commandment

"Honor your father and your mother, that your days may be long upon the land . . ."
                                                        Ex. 20:12

The family is a divine institution. God personally began the first family in the Garden of Eden when He presented Adam with his new wife Eve. We have already discussed the importance of the family. The institution of the family has a great responsibility. God has assigned the family with three important tasks: to propagate the human race, to teach children about God and to teach children about society. If the family fails in any one of these responsibilities, life on this planet would cease to exist as we know it. Clearly, the family has an enormous responsibility. Today the institution of the family is under attack by corrupt governments and extremist groups. Radical homosexuals want to redefine the family to include same sex marriage. This of course is against the natural order God has established for sex.

Homosexuality has nothing to offer anyone but disease and corruption. It is destructive to children and families. God wants families to be healthy and strong. A man and a woman who are committed to each other in holy matrimony can live their entire life free from sexually transmitted diseases. This is not likely to happen with homosexuality or with promiscuous heterosexuality.

At the time the Ten Commandments were written, the family had a far greater financial role than it does today. For example, consider the subject of retirement. Today, most retirements are funded by pension plans and by the government. The U.S. Government has a gigantic retirement system called the Social Security Administration. However, God has His own "Social Security Administration." It is called the family. To honor your father and your mother not only meant to respect them but to financially provide for them in their old age. God's retirement system has proven to be very successful. The family has an unparalleled record of success in providing for the elderly. The Ten Commandments support the family in a special way. God promises a long life to anyone who honors his parents. The Fifth Commandment is the only commandment which comes with this special promise. Interestingly, Jesus condemned a practice by some children who tried to escape their responsibility toward their parents. They would claim that money, which should have gone to their parents, was instead given to God as a gift. Of course, the claim was false. These children never actually gave their "gift" to God but kept it for themselves. Thus, the parents were denied the support that was rightfully theirs. See Matt. 15:1-9. If we want to honor God, let us honor our parents by providing for them when they are old and sick.

What have the Ten Commandments done for me? They gave me a family, the best Social Security System ever known to human history.

My Life: The Sixth Commandment

"You shall not murder."　　　Ex. 20:13

People want to live as long as possible. The desire to live seems to be universal. If you're interested in a long life, the Sixth Commandment is for you. If you want to live a long time, you need to do everything possible to stay healthy and to avoid behavior that can risk your life. Sexual sin for example is a behavior which can risk your life. Healthy living increases your chances of a long life. Additionally, other people must understand how important your life is. Other people must understand that your life has value. This is the purpose of the Sixth Commandment. It teaches us that human life has value. The reason we are commanded not to murder is because God created us. The Bible teaches us that every person was created in the "image" of God. See Gen. 1:26. God is the reason your life has value. Since God never changes, the value of your life can never change either. It does not matter whether you're intelligent, good looking or rich, nor does it matter how old or sick you are. Your life has unlimited value because you were made in the image of God. This is not only true for you individually but for everyone else as well.

Unfortunately, this commandment has been

misunderstood by some people. Some people translate the Sixth Commandment to say: "You shall not kill." As a result of this translation, they reason that capital punishment is wrong. They reason that capital punishment is a killing by the state and therefore violates the commandment. This view is incorrect. The intent of this commandment is to prohibit "murder." The Bible permits the taking of human life in certain circumstances. You can defend your life and your families' life with lethal force if necessary. The Bible permits capital punishment as well. This is clearly taught in Gen. 9:6 "Whoever sheds man's blood, By man his blood shall be shed; For in the image of God He made man." In the chapter following where the Ten Commandments are listed, capital punishment is even permitted if you strike or curse your parents. See Ex. 21: 15, 17.

The laws in the state where you live in prohibit murder. Murder is listed as a crime in the state penal code which the government will punish. Interestingly, our secular laws against murder originated from the Bible. The Sixth Commandment is the source for our modern laws against murder. Even the U.S. Supreme Court admits this is true. Consider what the U.S. Supreme Court said about the Decalogue. The word "Decalogue" is another term for the Ten Commandments. The word Decalogue is from two words, deka means "ten" and logos means "word." The Supreme Court said in 1960: "Innumerable civil regulations enforce conduct which harmonizes with religious canons. State prohibitions of murder, theft and adultery reinforce commands of the decalogue." Note 7. Thus, from the moment you were born, you have benefitted from this 3,500 year old commandment against murder. All of the tax money collected and spent on police protection to protect your life originated from the Ten Commandments! What have the Ten Commandments done for me? They have protected my life.

My Marriage: The Seventh Commandment

"You shall not commit adultery."

Ex. 20:14

If you are interested in having a successful marriage, this commandment is wise counsel. Nothing is more destructive to marriage than sexual sin. The key ingredients for a successful marriage are love and commitment. You must love your spouse in a way that you love no one else. Your love must be special and exclusive. Additionally, you must be committed to your spouse. Love and commitment are not the same thing. To be committed in a marriage relationship is to make a firm decision in your mind to cleave to your spouse no matter how you feel. It is separate from any feelings of love. It is a mental decision. Thus, even when you are angry with your spouse for a time and you don't feel much love for your partner, your commitment will carry you through. Sometimes marriages can be difficult. Relationships can be strained. This is when your commitment becomes important in keeping your marriage together. Finally, and most important, marriage is a three-way partnership. The partnership consists of a husband, a wife and God. God is the most important partner in any marriage. To have a successful marriage you need God. If a husband and wife love each other the way God loves them, their marriage can survive any difficulty that may arise. The more a couple love God, the stronger their marriage will be. The best barometer for the health of any marriage is how God fits into that marriage. Marriage partners who pray together will likely stay together.

At the time the Seventh Commandment was written polygamy was permitted. Thus, a man could have more than one wife and not be guilty of the sin of adultery. However, if a man had sex with another man's wife, they were both guilty of adultery. The punishment was death. See Lev. 20:10. Since New Testament times however, polygamy has not been permitted by God. This is because Jesus Christ as the Son of God restored the original intent God had for marriage. Jesus restored the relationship God intended for men and women to have before the Fall. Before the Fall, that is before Adam and Eve sinned, God intended one man to be married to one woman. The Bible says that the *two* shall become *one* flesh. See Matt. 19:5. A lifelong marriage between one woman and one man was the kind of relationship God intended. Jesus restored this relationship. Jesus did this in Matt. 5:32 and 19:9. What have the Ten Commandments done for me? They taught me how to have a happy and successful marriage.

My Property: The Eighth Commandment

"You shall not steal."   Ex. 20:15

Most people work very hard for what they get. The time they put into their jobs can never be replaced. How you spend one hour of your time is very important because you will never get that hour back. Once spent it is forever gone. Therefore, if you value your time, this commandment is important. Your right to own property comes from God. The government does not give you the right to own property. God gave it to you. The purpose of the government is to protect the property rights given to you by God. Since God gave us our rights to property, it is wrong for anyone to take our property from us. When a thief steals from you, he steals your time, he takes from you what God has given to you. Of course, in an ultimate sense, we never really "own" anything. Since God created the Universe, He owns everything, but God has established the institution of private property as the best way for people to produce the basic necessities of life like food, shelter and clothing. People will work hard if they can own what they earn. Private property provides an incentive for people to work harder and smarter. But there is an even more important reason for private property than just survival. When we work and create things, we share in the work of God. God worked and rested from His labor and so we should work and rest from our labor. The Bible says God put Adam in the Garden to "tend and keep it." See Gen. 2:15. This was Adam's job. He was to oversee the Garden of Eden, a great responsibility. What have the Ten Commandments done for me? They protect the one thing I never can replace, my time.

My Honesty: The Ninth Commandment

"You shall not bear false witness against your neighbor."   Ex. 20: 16

Stealing is a great sin to be sure, but the greatest theft in the world is a lie. Telling a lie about someone can cause irreparable damage. You might be able to recover stolen property but sometimes it's impossible to restore a reputation. Lies are very powerful things. They can cause more deaths than a thousand diseases. Millions of untold people have died because of lies. For example, the Nazi dictator and war criminal, Adolph Hitler bore false witness against his neighbors. He told the German people that they were better than their neighbors. He said that they were members of the master race. As a result of his lie, more than 50 million people died in World War II. One of the first sins recorded in the Bible was a lie. The Devil said in the Garden of Eden: "You will not surely die." Gen. 3:4. From the day this lie was believed, people have been dying ever since. If truth is important to you, then the Ninth Commandment should have great value for you. The only thing more powerful than a lie is the truth. Always tell the truth and expect the truth from others. To bear false witness against your neighbor not only refers to lying in court, but to lying anywhere. What have the Ten Commandments done for me? They protect me from lies and from the evil effects of a lie.

My Heart: The Tenth Commandment

"You shall not covet . . ."   Ex. 20:17

This commandment is different from the others in a special way. It is directed solely toward the heart. You can witness someone stealing something but sometimes it is very difficult to "see" someone committing covetousness. This sin is hidden in the heart, where all human sin originates. It is very important for us to keep our hearts pure. We must never open our hearts to bad thoughts and bad things. The best way to do this is to constantly fill our hearts with good thoughts. The Apostle Paul said "Finally, brethren, whatever things are true, whatever things are noble, whatever things are just, whatever things are pure, whatever things are lovely, whatever things are of good report, if there is any virtue and if there is anything praiseworthy–meditate on these things." Phil. 4:8. If we keep our hearts focused on good things and not give place to evil thoughts, we will avoid many of life's mistakes. [Special Note: the little book of Philippians in the New Testament is the best book in the world to teach us how to have good mental health.]

The Jewish interpretation of the Ten Commandments is interesting. The Jews not only divide the Ten Commandments into two groups of five but they cross aline them as well. For example, the First Commandment was lined up with the Sixth Commandment; the Second with the Seventh and so forth. The reasoning behind this is interesting. Consider the link between the First Commandment and the Sixth Commandment. The Jews believed that if you murdered someone, it is as though you murdered the Divine likeness. Since man was made in the image of God, if you commit murder, you have murdered the Divine likeness as well. Thus, to violate the Sixth Commandment is to violate the First Commandment as well. This is a fascinating way to view the Ten Commandments. What have the Ten Commandments done for me? They taught me to keep my heart pure. Note 8.

How the Ten Commandments Influenced American Law and Government

Our culture has an enormous impact on us. The way we think and how we think are to a large extent influenced by the culture we live in. Our approach to problems and how we solve them is affected by countless bits of information pouring into us from our environment. It has been said that people think "culturally." If this is true, then as members of the Western culture, we think in certain patterns so naturally that we are unaware we are doing it. Since the way we think is so natural to us, it is almost impossible for us to think in any other way. "Thinking outside the box" is a very difficult thing for people to do. The most important pattern of thought we have inherited as members of Western civilization is *monotheism*. Every child who is raised with Western values thinks like a monotheist. Virtually everyone reading this booklet thinks like a monotheist. You probably don't know you're doing it but it's true. As we shall see, it does not matter whether you believe in God or not. Atheists think like monotheists just the same. The celebrated atheist Madalyn Murray O'Hair spent her entire life thinking like a monotheist and she never knew it. Indeed, she was one of Moses' biggest fans albeit unknowingly. Members of the ACLU who believe in a strict separation of church and state-- think "religiously" every second of every day and they don't know they are doing it. Whether we like it or not, we live in a cultural box, and the No. 1 concept in our cultural box is "monotheism." Without question, the most important concept that makes our civilization "Western" civilization is monotheism. Monotheism tops the list of core values of Western nations, and whenever you talk about "monotheism," you must talk about the Ten Commandments! The Ten Commandments are the glue that binds our society to monotheism. Without the Ten Commandments, Western societies would be very different from what they are today. This is why it is impossible to overstate the importance of the Ten Commandments to Western law and government. The Ten Commandments not only influenced our religion but the way we *think*.

How the Ten Commandments
Influenced the Declaration of Independence

Let's consider an example of how monotheism influenced Western law and government. Consider the Declaration of Independence written by Thomas Jefferson in 1776. The Declaration of Independence is the moral and philosophical foundation for a free and independent government in the United States. The Declaration of Independence explains how America came to be. Its words are the "guts of America." In the Declaration of Independence, Jefferson made the case for independence from the British Empire. The moral foundation for the American Revolution according to Thomas Jefferson was monotheism. Monotheism was the ultimate justification to take up arms against the British government and establish the Government of the United States. This is true because in the Declaration of Independence, Jefferson appealed to *certain universal moral principles that are true for all time for all peoples everywhere.* These universal moral principles are possible in only one system of thought: monotheism. The following words by Jefferson appeal to monotheism as justification for the American Revolution:

"When in the Course of human events, it becomes necessary for one people to dissolve the political bands which have connected them with another, and to assume among the Powers of the earth, the separate and equal station to which the Laws of Nature and of Nature's God entitle them, a decent respect to the opinions of mankind requires that they should declare the causes which impel them to the separation.

We hold these truths to be self-evident, that all men are created equal, that they are endowed by their Creator with certain unalienable Rights, that among these are Life, Liberty and the pursuit of Happiness. That to secure these rights, Governments are instituted among Men, deriving their just powers from the consent of the governed. That whenever any Form of Government becomes destructive of these ends, it is the Right of the People to alter or to abolish it, and to institute new Government . . ." The Declaration of Independence.

To help us see the concept of monotheism in the Declaration of Independence, let's take another journey back in time. Let's go back to the time when the Ten Commandments were written. Let's go back to 3,500 years ago when the world was dominated by polytheism. The gods were everywhere. There was a god for every kingdom, empire, city and village. Indeed, there was a god for every mountain, valley, river and lake. Many animals were gods as well. Now let's assume you want to take a journey. You want to travel from Greece to Egypt and then to Persia. Every time you change your location, you meet new gods. When you leave Greece, you leave behind the Greek gods. When you come to Egypt, you come to the Egyptian gods, and when you arrive in Persia, you will meet the Persian gods. Meeting new gods can cause problems. In the ancient world, each god was entitled to make his or her own laws. This meant that the gods of Greece had one set of laws, the gods of

Egypt another set of laws and so forth. Thus, the law could change a lot depending upon the gods. This view of the law had a profound impact on government and basic human rights. Since there were many different gods, there were many different laws. Consequently, your rights as a human being changed each time you came to a new god. Human rights were *relative*. Thus, the rights the gods of Greece will allow might not be the same in Egypt or in Persia. In other words, in the ancient world, the concept of universal human rights did not exist. There was no such thing as a human right which was true for every person no matter where he or she lived. The system of polytheism would not allow for the existence of universal human rights. Now let's change the equation. Suppose there is only One God making all the laws. Instead of many gods making many different laws, suppose there is only One God making all the laws. What would the effect be? The effect on human rights is profound. Instead of human rights being relative they now become *absolute*. Your rights will not change every time you change your location. Your rights will be the same in Greece or in Egypt or in Persia. There is one universal standard of human rights for all peoples everywhere. This is what the Ten Commandments gave us. No matter where you are, or what millennium you live in, every person has certain fundamental rights. You have a fundamental right to life and liberty.

The influence of the Ten Commandments on the Declaration of Independence is now obvious. When Jefferson said that there are certain truths which are self-evident, "We hold these truths to be self-evident" he must believe that a self-evident truth is always true. It does not matter whether you live in 1776 or not. A self-evident truth is always true. The only possible foundation for Jefferson's self-evident truth was monotheism. Jefferson must find a source for his self-evident truth. The only way his self-evident truth could exist is to believe that there is a Creator who transcends time. The belief in an all-powerful Creator who is not limited by time or space made his self-evident truth possible. This is why Jefferson linked self-evident truth with the Creator, "We hold these truths to be self-evident, that all men are created equal, that they are endowed by their Creator with certain unalienable Rights." When Jefferson referred to the Creator, he was making a direct appeal to monotheism. The only way you can have a truth that is always true regardless of time is to have One Creator God, who has one law and one absolute truth. By definition, polytheism will not permit a single truth to exist. In a system of polytheism, there are as many "truths" as there are gods. The concept of universal truth was impossible in polytheism. However, in monotheism it is possible. Thus, the Ten Commandments had a profound influence on the Declaration of Independence. Admittedly, there may have been other religions in history which taught a form of monotheism as well. However, they all pale in comparison to Moses and the Ten Commandments. Without the Ten Commandments, Jefferson's Declaration of Independence would not have been possible. Additionally, there can be no question that when Jefferson used the word "Creator" in the Declaration of Independence, he was referring to the Creator of the Holy Bible and the Ten Commandments. This is proved by Jefferson's historic *"A Bill for Establishing Religious Freedom"* which he wrote three years after he wrote the Declaration of Independence. In this bill, which was intended to protect the freedom of religion in Virginia, Jefferson used biblical terms like "Almighty God" "Holy author of our religion" and "Lord both of body and mind." Jefferson's bill was finally passed in 1786. Thus, the monotheistic deity found in Jefferson's *"A Bill for Establishing Religious Freedom"* was the same deity for the Declaration of Independence. Note 9.

How the Ten Commandments Influenced the U.S. Constitution

If you believe that every citizen should be treated equally under the law, you should thank Moses for this. If you believe that every word in the U.S. Constitution belongs to every American equally, you owe this belief to the Ten Commandments. If you believe that the value of one human life is no less or greater than any other human life, then you're a monotheist. It does not matter whether you believe in God or not, if you accept any of these ideas you support the key concepts of monotheism. Most Americans are unaware of just how popular Moses is in the United States. Moses is popular in America because he gave us our concept of equality. Unfortunately, many people do not know that he did this. I am always amazed by people who think that the Constitution is a "secular" document or a "godless" document. No doubt you have heard that the word "God" is not in the Constitution and that this proves that the United States should be a secular state. The reality is, God is in every word of the Constitution, including the punctuation! People who think that "God" is not in the Constitution simply because the word is not there reveal just how little they understand it. Below the surface of the words in the Constitution, there are a mountain of ideas which made its formation possible. The No. 1 idea embedded in the Constitution was monotheism. The U.S. Constitution would not be possible but for Moses and the monotheism he taught in the Ten Commandments. Let's consider why this is true. Note 10.

    Equal Justice Under Law. If Moses stood before the U.S. Supreme Court today and saw the words *Equal Justice Under Law* on the building, he would be very pleased. He would be pleased to know how far his ideas have gone. The concept of *Equal Justice Under Law* is an exclusively religious concept; it did not originate from secularism. (As we shall see, one of the key pillars of secularism is the theory of evolution. Historically, the theory of evolution was very hostile to the idea of human equality.) When the U.S. Supreme Court chose to put the words *Equal Justice Under Law* on the outside wall, they unknowingly chose a message every bit as religious as "salvation from sin" or "You must be born again." Although the word "God" does not appear, the phrase *Equal Justice Under Law* is a religious message none the less because religion was its inspiration. To see how Moses and the Ten Commandments contributed to human equality, let's take another journey back in time. Let's go back to the time when the Ten Commandments were written. If there was one prevailing characteristic of the ancient world, it was inequality. Human beings were anything but equal. The idea that every person was equal under the law did not exist. The gods not only had many laws but they had different laws for different groups of people. The gods favored some groups over others. The gods favored the rulers over the slaves, the priests over the laity, and men over women. Thus, the ancient world was a very unequal place. Even today the superiority of one group of people over another continues to exist. In India, human inequality is rampant due to the caste system. There are 3,000 different castes in India with 25,000 sub castes. Thus, the system of polytheism made human beings unequal.

Then Moses came with a revolutionary new idea: the idea that there is only One God. Most important in his teachings concerning this One God is the belief that He is sole Creator of the human race. The Bible says "And the Lord God formed man of the dust of the ground, and breathed into his nostrils the breath of life; and man became a living being." Gen. 2:7. The Bible teaches that all humanity came from one man and one woman. The entire human race can be traced back to one man named Adam and one woman named Eve. By definition, this means that all individuals are equal regardless of race or sex. Human beings are equal because they all descended from the same parents. The American concept of human equality is based on this teaching found in the Bible. Thus, the system of monotheism with One God as the sole Creator made human equality possible as well as equal justice under the law. The reader will recall that the Fourth Commandment in the Ten Commandments concerns the Sabbath. The Sabbath is a celebration of the Lord God as the Creator. Clearly, the Ten Commandments affirm the idea of One Creator and therefore human equality. When considered in this light, the observation by secularists that the word "God" is not in the Constitution is rather shallow. The Constitution would not be possible but for the Ten Commandments and the monotheism it taught.

The Abolition of Slavery. It is an undisputed fact that religion led to the end of slavery in the United States. Consider the oldest written constitution still in force, the Massachusetts Constitution of 1780, which refers to "the great Creator and Preserver of the Universe." In Article 1, it discussed the equality of the human race and said: "All men are born free and equal, and have certain natural, essential, and unalienable rights . . . " In 1783, Chief Justice Cushing of the Massachusetts Supreme Court used these words to ban slavery in Massachusetts. This was more than 80 years before the U.S. Constitution would ban slavery in the United States. Note 11. In 1833, the Abolitionists movement in America was spear headed by people who believed that slavery was a sin. The Constitution of the American Anti-Slavery Society overtly referred to biblical values to attack slavery. The first sentence of their constitution said: "Whereas the Most High

God 'hath made of one blood all nations of men . . . and whereas, our National Existence is based upon this principle, as recognized in the Declaration of Independence . . . The object of this Society is the entire abolition of Slavery in the United States." Note 12. The influence of religious values in the U.S. Constitution came with the passage of the Thirteenth, Fourteenth and Fifteenth Amendments, sometimes called the Civil War Amendments. The Thirteenth Amendment outlawed slavery in the United States. The Fifteenth Amendment protected the right of African American men to vote. The Fourteenth Amendment gave African American men and women the status of citizenship in the United States. It also gave them the equality Moses taught in the Ten Commandments by adding an Equal Protection Clause. The Fourteenth Amendment in Article 1 says: "nor deny to any person within its jurisdiction the equal protection of the laws." Sometimes people think the Bible approves of slavery. This view is not correct. The institution of slavery was the result of human sin. God did not intend slavery to exist. Slavery is like divorce in some ways. God hates divorce because it destroys families. However, God allowed it under certain circumstances because of the "hardness of your hearts." Matt. 19:8. Merely because God recognized that slavery and divorce exists, this should not be interpreted to mean that God approves of it. God intended every human being to be free just like Adam and Eve.

Charles Darwin verses Moses. In modern times, the biggest challenger to human equality was Charles Darwin. When Darwin proposed his theory of evolution, the No. 1 idea he attacked was the view that God created the Universe. Consequently, there are two views to explain the existence of the Universe today. There is the theory of evolution and the creationist view. Most people are aware of the great debate between the evolutionists and the creationists. However, most people are unaware of the second idea that Darwin attacked. The No. 2 idea that Darwin attacked was the belief that human beings were equal. Historically, evolutionists were hostile to the idea of human equality. In the past, evolutionists believed that some human races were superior to others. Darwin's title to his book suggests the superiority of some races. The full title of Darwin's historic book is: *The Origin of Species by Means of Natural Selection or the Preservation of Favored Races in the Struggle for Life.* Notice the key words: *"Preservation"* and *"Favored Races."* Most people are unaware of the link between racism and evolution. Toward the end of the 19th and during the early part of the 20th century, the scientific community was dominated by the "theory of eugenics" or as it is sometimes called Social Darwinism. The theory of eugenics, a theory that Darwin himself did not promote but his followers (including his son), believed that you could develop a race of human beings intellectually superior and free from disease. Eugenicists believed that through the proper administration of the nation's gene pool, a superior race of human beings could be created. Today, the global competition among the nations of the world is seen in terms of economic growth, military might, and technology. At the turn of the 20th century, it was seen in terms of genetics as well. The nation with the best genes will be the winner of the global competition. Consequently, the United States and many other nations began to pass laws to force the sterilization of the "feeble minded" "criminals" and "alcoholics." Sadly, the theory of eugenics dominated American law. The most famous case by the U.S. Supreme Court which supported the theory of eugenics was called *Buck v. Bell* decided in 1927. Note 13. Nazi war criminals cited the *Buck v. Bell* case to justify their sterilization programs in the Third Reich. Note 14. American education taught the theory of eugenics as well. The celebrated Scopes trial of 1925 was about the teaching of evolution in the public schools of Tennessee. What is generally not known about the case is that the text book used by John Scopes in his biology class was titled *A Civic Biology*. The author was George William Hunter. Hunter's text book taught the superiority of the white race based on the theory of evolution. Note 15. This poses an interesting question: in 1925, which side was really backward in their thinking? The side which supported creationism and the equality of the human race or the evolutionists who taught the superiority of the white race based on science? Thankfully, post World War II evolutionists have repudiated the theory of eugenics. The horrors of the Nazi death camps exposed the dangers of eugenics. Note 16.

The Rights of Women. The monotheism of the Ten Commandments had an important impact on the rights of women as well. The women's movement in America was spear headed by people who believed that sexism was a sin. Just as the Abolitionists cited "the Creator" in the Declaration of Independence to justify their cause, so did the members of the women's movement. In 1848, at the historic Seneca Falls Convention in New York, the delegates adopted a "Declaration of Sentiments and Resolutions" modeled after Jefferson's Declaration of Independence. The second paragraph said: "We hold these truths to be self-evident: that all men and women are created equal; that they are endowed by their Creator with certain inalienable rights . . . " One of the "Resolutions" said: "Resolved, That woman is man's equal–was intended to be so by the Creator . . . " This religious fervor for women's rights ultimately found expression in the U.S. Constitution with the passage of the Nineteenth Amendment in 1920. Here the right of women to vote was protected. Sometimes some people think the Bible discriminates against women. This view is not correct. As the "Declaration of Sentiments and Resolutions" said, it was the "perverted application of the Scriptures" which caused the abuse of women, not the Bible. It was men who "usurped the prerogative of Jehovah himself" which denied women their rights, not God. Note 17. Many people are aware that the New Testament says that Jesus first appeared to women after His resurrection. Few people however, understand the significance of this event. Under traditional Jewish law only men could be witnesses in court or to any event. The rabbinic law discriminated against women. When Jesus appeared to women as the first witnesses of His resurrection, He was in effect teaching us that women should have the same rights under the law as men. He was teaching us that women were equal to men before God. Jesus Christ is the true liberator of women.

The Freedom of Religion. If you believe that the leaders of government should serve the people and not vice versa, you should thank Moses for this. The Ten Commandments had an enormous impact on the freedom of religion in America. To understand why this is true, let's take another journey back in time. Let's go back 3,500 years ago to when the Lord gave the First Commandment: "You shall have no other gods before Me." We have already learned that ancient peoples believed in polytheism, in many gods. However, in the ancient world, it was possible for a human being to be a god as well. In many instances, the political leaders depended upon religion for their authority to rule the people. They depended upon the common belief that the political ruler was a god. In effect, the institution of the state was god and it was the duty of the people to serve the state accordingly. Any opposition to the state was not only a political offense but a religious offense as well. Ancient Egypt is a good example of how the leaders of government and religion were combined. In ancient Egypt, the Pharaohs were believed to be the living incarnation of the sun god Ra, Egypt's most important god. When Pharaoh died, he returned back to the sun from which he came. The ancient Romans worshiped the Caesars as gods as well. In 44 B.C., Augustus Caesar pointed to a great comet that appeared over Rome that year and said that this comet was a sign that Julius Caesar, his uncle was elevated to the ranks of the gods. It should be obvious that the belief that the government and the gods were the same thing totally eliminated any possibility of political and religious freedom for the people. The main obstacle to religious freedom in the ancient world was THE GOVERNMENT. Then Moses came with his teaching of monotheism in the Ten Commandments. When he taught that there was only One God, it had a powerful impact on politics as well. Monotheism completely destroyed the idea that the state and its rulers were gods. In effect, monotheism separated God from the institutions of government. Monotheism not only stripped the government of all heavenly powers but made the government subject to Heaven as well. It made government a servant of the people. This view of government influenced Thomas Jefferson. In his Declaration of Independence, Jefferson said: "That to secure these rights, (The rights given to us by the Creator) Governments are instituted among Men, deriving their just powers from the consent of the governed, That whenever any Form of Government becomes destructive of these ends, it is the Right of the People to alter or to abolish it, and to institute new Government . . . " It is not an exaggeration to say that the most powerful influence for religious and political freedom in history was the Ten Commandments.

Should Religious Values Influence the U.S. Constitution?

As we have seen, from the beginning religious values have influenced the U.S. Constitution. Religion played an important part in the formation of the U.S. Constitution. The American concept of *Equal Justice Under Law* is the result of the influence of religion. The desire to protect the freedom of religion, African Americans and women all had their genesis in monotheism. Secularist groups like the ACLU who argue that religion should not influence the U.S. Constitution are woefully ignorant of how important monotheism is to American law. Thankfully, Americans in the past did not believe what the ACLU does today. The American people passed the Civil War Amendments and the Nineteenth Amendment because they believed that their faith demanded it. If religion did not have the kind of influence it had on 19th century America, it is possible that slavery and the subjugation of women might not have ended when it did. Even the First Amendment to the Bill of Rights, which protects the freedom of religion in America, was passed for religious reasons. The First Amendment was passed to insure that the Federal Government could never claim the kind of loyalty that belongs only to God. The historical evidence suggests that religious values should influence the U.S. Constitution.

Should the Ten Commandments be Displayed on Public Property? What About Judge Roy Moore?

On November 13, 2003, Chief Justice Roy Moore of the Alabama Supreme Court was removed from office. Judge Moore had refused to obey a court order issued by Judge Myron Thompson of the U.S. District Court for the Middle District of Alabama to remove a Ten Commandments Monument from the rotunda of the State Judicial Building. The dispute began on August 1, 2001, when Judge Moore installed a 5,200 lb. monument which displayed the Ten Commandments as well as quotes from the Declaration of Independence, the Constitution of Alabama, the National Motto and other quotes. After various appeals, the Ten Commandments Monument was finally removed from the rotunda on August 27, 2003. We are told that the display of the Ten Commandments on public property violated the First Amendment. This is nonsense.

Reasonable people may disagree about the wisdom of displaying the Ten Commandments on public property. Personally, I think it is a great idea. But from a legal standpoint there can be no question about its constitutionality. The framers of the U.S. Constitution and the framers of the First Amendment intended all issues concerning religion to be left to the states. If the framers of the First Amendment were alive today, they would tell us that this issue should be left to the states and that federal courts and federal judges should not be involved. They would tell us that the state constitution and state laws should decide this issue, not the First Amendment. The framers would tell us that each state is free to decide for itself whether it will or will not allow the display of the Ten Commandments on public property. From 1791, when the First Amendment was ratified to 1940, this was the rule in the United States. Federal judges were never involved in these kinds of issues. Consequently, prior to1940, there are no examples of a federal judge ordering a state judge to remove a Ten Commandments display.

Sadly in 1940, the rule was changed. In 1940, the U.S. Supreme Court claimed that the Fourteenth Amendment changed the old rule. They claimed that the Fourteenth Amendment made the religion clauses in the First Amendment applicable to the states. They made this claim in a case called *Cantwell v. Connecticut*. Note 18. The Cantwells were Jehovah's Witnesses who were fined for soliciting donations and distributing religious materials in New Haven, Connecticut without a license. The U.S. Supreme Court said that these fines by the State of Connecticut violated the First Amendment to the Constitution. This was new. There are two religion clauses in the First Amendment. There is an Establishment Clause and a Free Exercise Clause. The Establishment Clause says: "Congress shall make no law respecting an establishment of religion . . . " The Free Exercise Clause says: ". . . or prohibiting the free exercise thereof" In the *Cantwell* case, the Supreme Court said that the fines violated the Free Exercise Clause. In the case involving Judge Roy

Moore, the courts said that the display of the Ten Commandments violated the Establishment Clause.

The courts in Judge Moore's case are wrong for three reasons. First, the Supreme Court's claim that the First Amendment has jurisdiction over the states is not correct. The First Amendment does not have jurisdiction over a state government. Jurisdiction refers to where a law has power or authority. The Fourteenth Amendment did not change the First Amendment or its jurisdiction. Since the religion clauses in the First Amendment do not apply to a state, U.S. District Judge Myron Thompson did not have one ounce of legal authority to order Judge Moore to do anything with the Ten Commandments. The Supreme Court's claim that the Fourteenth Amendment made the First Amendment applicable to the states is a sham. The Supreme Court made this claim for one reason, to grab more power for themselves. The fact that the Supreme Court did not make this claim concerning the First Amendment until 72 years after the Fourteenth Amendment was ratified (1868) is compelling evidence against it. [1940 - 1868 = 72]. Even the ACLU will admit that the framers of the First Amendment intended to limit the jurisdiction of the First Amendment to the Federal Government. Second, even if we assume that the Supreme Court is correct and that the First Amendment has jurisdiction over a state, the display of the Ten Commandments would not violate the Establishment Clause. There can be no question that the framers of the First Amendment would allow the display of the Ten Commandments on public property. The reader will recall that James Madison, six months before he attended the constitutional convention in Philadelphia, passed a Sabbath law in Virginia. Madison as a member of the Virginia legislature, successfully passed a Sabbath law in November 1786 and then attended the constitutional convention from May to September 1787. (See comments above concerning "My Creator: The Fourth Commandment.") If James Madison, who sponsored the First Amendment in Congress, would pass a state law which fined anyone who violated the Sabbath, then it is logical to conclude that he would not oppose the display of the Ten Commandments which listed the Sabbath commandment. Clearly, the framers of the First Amendment would not oppose the public acknowledgment of God such as a Ten Commandments display. Note 19. Regrettably, the Supreme Court has rejected the views of James Madison and the framers of the First Amendment. They have adopted a very extremist interpretation of the First Amendment. This has been particularly true since the 1960's. Rather than protect the freedom of religion in America, the Supreme Court has used the First Amendment to promote an attitude of intolerance toward religion. Consequently, the Supreme Court has divided the American people over religion more than any religious institution or cult in history. No one divides America over religion more than the Supreme Court. Absolutely, no one.

Third, let us for a moment put aside the legal debate concerning Judge Roy Moore and the controversy in Alabama. Can there be any doubt that a display of the Ten Commandments on public property is consistent with America's spiritual heritage? It is an undisputed fact that this nation was founded by people looking for religious freedom. Almost all of the American colonies were founded by people looking for religious freedom. A casual reading of the Mayflower Compact will prove how true this is. Indeed, the first promise of America was the freedom of religion for all pilgrims. The spiritual heritage of America is confirmed by George Washington in his Farewell Address of 1796 and by Abraham Lincoln in his Gettysburg Address and in many other events in our national history. The spiritual character of the American people is confirmed by the prayer that President Roosevelt led the nation in on D-day, June 6, 1944. For any court to hold that the display of the Ten Commandments offends the U.S. Constitution is a violation of American history. Sadly, groups like the ACLU and many federal courts do not like our national heritage. They reject the moral and spiritual values that made America great. They even reject many of the principles found in the Constitution. Note 20. They want to remold America into a radical secularist state. Consequently, they have a very intolerant attitude toward religion. I hope you, dear reader, will not support their efforts. I hope you will embrace our national heritage and support the freedom of religion in America. I hope you will support Judge Roy Moore and the display of the Ten Commandments. Blessings to you.

END NOTES.

Note 1. The verse concerning God's Word not returning to Him void is found in Isa. 55:11. The story of the woman with the disease is found in Matt. 9:18-26; Mk. 5:21-34; Lk. 8:40-44.

Note 2. Isaac Landman, ed., Vol. 8., The Universal Jewish Encyclopedia, Hirschel Revel, *Noahide Laws*, p. 227 (1948). The reader is advised that the order for the Noahide Laws may vary depending upon the source.

Note 3. Zev Vilnay, Legends of Galilee, Jordan and Sinai, *Why Was The Holy Law Given In A Wilderness?* p. 351 (1978).

Note 4. The key verse in the Old Testament is Deuteronomy 6:4. This verse is about monotheism. Dt. 6:4 says "Hear, O Israel: the Lord our God, the Lord is one!" This verse is actually a prayer called the Shema, from the Hebrew word "to hear." In traditional Jewish households the Shema is the first thing a child is taught to speak. Traditional Jews place an extra emphasis on the word "one" when saying the prayer. Also, the Shema is the last thing a traditional Jew will speak before death. See the Code of Jewish Law by Rabbi Solomon Ganzfried, editor, and Hyman E. Goldin, translator, for various customs concerning the Shema. Many Christians would consider Jno. 3:16 to be the key verse in the New Testament. This verse is known as "The Gospel Verse."

Note 5. Justice Felix Frankfurter in a concurring opinion said the following: "Legislation currently in force in forty-nine of the fifty States illegalizes on Sunday some form of conduct lawful if performed on weekdays. In several States only one or a few activities are banned—the sale of alcoholic beverages, hunting, barbering, pawnbroking . . . –but thirty-four jurisdictions broadly ban Sunday labor, or the employment of labor . . . " See *McGowan v. Maryland,* 366 U.S. 420 at 495 (1960). Apparently, Alaska was the only state not to have a Sunday or Sabbath law.

Note 6. Julian P. Boyd, ed., Vol. 2. , The Papers of Thomas Jefferson, Princeton University Press, (1950). This publication by Princeton University is the most authoritative collection of Jefferson's writings in existence. For Bill No. 84, *A Bill for Punishing Disturbers of Religious Worship and Sabbath Breakers,* see p. 555.

Note 7. *McGowan v. Maryland* at 462.

Note 8. For an interesting discussion of how the Ten Commandments cross line-up, see <u>Aseres Hadibros/The Ten Commandments</u> by Rabbi Avrohom Chaim Feuer & Rabbi Nosson Scherman, p. 54-61; Published by Mesorah Publications, Ltd.:The ArtScroll Mesorah Series (1981).

Note 9. Vol. 2. , <u>The Papers of Thomas Jefferson</u>, for Bill No. 82, *A Bill for Establishing Religious Freedom*, see p. 545. On his tombstone, Jefferson wanted to be remembered for three things, a) the authorship of the Declaration of Independence, b) the founding of the University of Virginia and c) Bill No. 82, *A Bill for Establishing Religious Freedom.*

Note 10. Interestingly, the divine reference in the U.S. Constitution to "our Lord" in Article 7, is not important to secularists. They generally dismiss it as a mere formality. However, the historical evidence suggests that this may be a mistake. One state supreme court has held that the reference to "Lord" in Article 7 is a direct reference to Jesus Christ. In 1915, the Louisiana Supreme Court claimed that because the word "Lord" was preceded by the word "our" that this must refer to Jesus Christ. The Louisiana Supreme Court cited an identical reference in the Articles of Confederation to justify their view. See *Herold v. Parish Board of School Directors*, 136 L.R. 1034 at 1044 (1915).

Note 11. Henry Steele Commager & Richard B. Morris, editors., <u>The Spirit of 'Seventy-Six</u>, *Massachusetts Puts An End To Slavery-1783*, p. 406. (1958). The case was *Commonwealth v. Nathaniel Jennison*. Chief Justice Cushing of Massachusetts who wrote the decision would later be appointed to serve on the first U.S. Supreme Court by George Washington.

Note 12. Henry Steele Commager, ed., <u>Documents of American History,</u> *The American Anti-Slavery Society: Constitution And Declaration of Sentiments,* December 4, 1833, p. 278 (1943).

Note 13. *Buck v. Bell*, 274 U.S. 200 at 207 (1927) Justice Oliver Wendell Holmes writing for the Court said: "We have seen more than once that the public welfare may call upon the best citizens for their lives. It would be strange if it could not call upon those who already sap the strength of the State for these lesser sacrifices, often not felt to be such by those concerned, in order to prevent our being swamped with incompetence. It is better for all the world, if instead of waiting to execute degenerate offspring for crime, or to let them starve for their imbecility, society can prevent those who are manifestly unfit from continuing their kind. The principle that sustains compulsory vaccination is broad enough to cover cutting the Fallopian tubes. . . Three generations of imbeciles are enough."

Note 14. Edward W. Knappman, ed. <u>American Trials of the 20th Century,</u> (1994). On page 122 the author said: "After World War II, defending the forcible sterilization of 2 million people, lawyers for Nazi war criminals cited this law [Virginia's sterilization law in Buck v. Bell] and pointed out that the U.S. Supreme Court, in Buck v. Bell, had declared such laws constitutional." [Added].

Note 15. George William Hunter,<u> A Civic Biology</u> (1914). On page 196 Hunter said: "**The Races of Man.**—At the present time there exist upon the earth five races or varieties of man, each very different from the other in instincts, social customs, and, to an extent, in structure. These are the Ethiopian or negro type, originating in Africa; the Malay or brown race, from the islands of the Pacific; the American Indian; the Mongolian or yellow race, including the natives of China, Japan, and the Eskimos; and finally, the highest type of all, the Caucasians, represented by the civilized white inhabitants of Europe and America."

Note 16. The <u>Dictionary of the History of Science</u> defined eugenics this way:

"**eugenics.** A social movement holding that human mental and physical characters are heritable, and that steps should be taken to ensure the race is constantly genetically improved. It is conventional to refer to negative eugenics–which stops persons with 'undesirable' traits from reproducing–and positive eugenics –which encourages the reproduction of 'desirable' types [environmental–heredity controversy.]

Eugenic ideas may be detected as early as Plato (427-347 BC), but eugenics became significant only after the publication of Charles Darwin's (1809-82) *Origin of Species* (1859), which implied that man was the outcome of a natural process of evolution. Francis Galton (1822-1911), who coined the term, from the 1870's combined research into human heredity and human intelligence with a campaign on behalf of eugenic breeding. From 1900 popular eugenics movements and centres for eugenic study were set up in Britain, America, Germany, the Soviet Union and elsewhere. The social effects of the movements varied enormously from country to country and, in some cases, it is hard to separate the effects of eugenics from those of unthinking racism. Since the demise of Nazism, eugenics has generally been viewed with suspicion." See W.F. Bynum, E.J. Browne, Roy Porter, editors, <u>Dictionary of the History of Science,</u> p. 131, Princeton University Press, (1981).

Charles Darwin's son, Major Leonard Darwin of Her Majesty's Royal Engineers served as president of the Eugenics Society in England from 1891 to 1928. See Pat Shipman, <u>The Evolution of Racism,</u> p. 121 (1994). Also, Leonard Darwin presided over the first International Congress for Eugenics held in London in 1912. See Stefan Kuhl, <u>The Nazi Connection, Eugenics, American Racism, and German National Socialism</u>, p. 13-14 (1994).

For an excellent discussion of the link between Darwinism and master race ideology see "Darwinism and the Nazi race Holocaust" at http://www.answersingenesis.org/docs/4162.asp Also see http://www.lifesite.net/waronfamily/Population_Control/Inheren tracism.pdf

Note 17. <u>Documents of American History</u>, *"Woman's Rights,"* p. 315.

Note 18. *Cantwell v. Connecticut*, 310 U.S. 296 (1940). As a result of this case, the states were for the first time required to follow the religion clauses in the First Amendment, which meant of course that from now on the Federal Government would control religion law in the United States. Thus, the first time the First Amendment was used in a school prayer case was not until 1950, after *Cantwell* was decided.

Note 19. See my article "Would Thomas Jefferson Display the Ten Commandments?'

For Part 1 go to:

http://www.faithandaction.org/DavidNewFeb04.htm

For Part 2 go to:

http://www.faithandaction.org/DavidNewMarch04.htm

Note 20. See *"The Principle of Enumeration Abandoned"* in <u>The Constitution for Beginners</u> by David W. New, Esq. For ordering information go to www.myconstitution.us

RECOMMENDED READING:

The Ten Words That Will Change A Nation: The Ten Commandments by Robert L. Schenck. For ordering information call 202-546-8329 or go to www.faithandaction.org. This work is an excellent study of the Ten Commandments.

CONTACT AND ORDERING INFORMATION

Contact and Ordering Information for publications
by David W. New:

The Ten Commandments for Beginners
$4.95 per copy
For details about this booklet, visit:
                                    www.mytencommandments.us

Religious Freedom in America for Beginners
$4.95 per copy
For details about this booklet, visit: www.religiousfreedom.us

The First Amendment and the Bill of Rights for Beginners
$4.95 per copy
For details about this booklet, visit: www.myfirstamendment.us

The Constitution for Beginners
$4.95 per copy
For details about this booklet, visit: www.myconstitution.us

Make Checks Or Money Orders Payable To:
David W. New

Mail Orders To:
David W. New

Attorney at Law

6701 Democracy Blvd.   For Shipping And Handling ADD
Suite 300   For 1 to 3 copies add $1.50
Bethesda, MD 20817   For 4 to 9 copies add $2.50
301-468-4905   For 10 copies or more: FREE

Maryland Residents Only:
Add 5% Sales Tax

Email Address:
david_new@msn.com